W9-AKD-966

J
133.1   Salzer, L.E.
Sa   Haunted house mysteries

DATE DUE

OCT. 20 1984	AP 25 '88	MY 30 '91
OCT. 25 1984	JY 27 '88	AG 8 '91
NOV. 14 1984	SE 21 '88	SE 12 '91
DEC. 26 1984	AP 10 '89	
	OC 19 '89	MR 26 '92
FEB. 09 1985	OC 30 '89	MY 19 '92
MAR. 4 1985	NO 10 '89	JY 3 '92
MR 17 '86	FE 2 '90	JY 23 '92
JY 25 '86	MR 23 '90	NO 19 '92
FE 18 '87	AP 25 '90	JUN 27 '93
SE 2 '87	JE 1 '90	AUG 17 '94
	OC 24 '90	SEP 06 '94
		MR 21 01

DEMCO

Haunted House Mysteries

by L.E. Salzer

cpi
contemporary perspectives, inc.

This book is distributed by Silver Burdett Company, Morristown, New Jersey 07960.

Library of Congress Number: 78-10951

Art and Photo Credits
Cover Photo, courtesy of Lionel Wilson
Illustrations on pages 5, 9, 13, 14, 23, 25, 35, and 48, Jon Gampert
Illustrations on pages 13, 14, 23, 25, 41, and 48, courtesy of Coronet Instructional
Media, a division of Esquire, Inc.
Photos on pages 17 and 19, The Granger Collection, New York
Photo on page 21, by gracious permission of Her Majesty Queen Elizabeth II
Photo on page 27, British Crown copyright
Photo on page 28, courtesy of Lionel Wilson
Photos on pages 31 and 38, The Bettmann Archive
Photo on page 37, Photoworld, Inc.
Illustration on page 41, Gerald Smith
Photos on pages 43 and 45, courtesy of the Winchester Mystery House

Library of Congress Cataloging in Publication Data

Salzer, L	E	1930-
Haunted house mysteries		

SUMMARY: Discusses ghosts purportedly present at
Hampton Court Palace, Winchester Ghost Mansion, and
Octagon House.
    1. Ghosts — Juvenile literature. [1. Ghosts]
I. Title.
BF1461.S33   133.1'22   78-10951
ISBN 0-89547-070-5

Manufactured in the United States of America
ISBN 0-89547-070-5

Contents

Chapter 1
The Tenant in the Attic   4

Chapter 2
Ghosts on Parade   11

Chapter 3
The Haunted Gallery   16

Chapter 4
The Ghost of Octagon House   29

Chapter 5
Guest House for Ghosts   39

What Do *You* Think?   48

The Tenant in the Attic

Have you ever wondered what it's like to meet a ghost?

Margie Walker never wondered — but she found out!

It was a hot summer afternoon. Margie climbed the steps to the attic of her house. Margie had never been in the attic. Now she wondered what was there. All her friends had found strange old things in their attics.

Margie reached the attic door. She pushed, but nothing moved. She pushed again — very hard. But still the door didn't move an inch!

Then suddenly, with a loud scraping noise, the heavy door opened by itself! One short step and Margie was inside.

But now she stopped. Something was wrong. On this very hot summer day, the little room was damp

and cold. The cold seemed strange too. It wasn't like any cold Margie had ever known. She felt as if it were *touching* her. It seemed to wrap itself around her like a blanket of ice.

Margie was shaking — and not only from the cold. She was afraid!

Then she told herself there really wasn't anything to be afraid of. After all, the cold must have been only a sudden change in the weather.

Besides, she forgot about it as soon as she looked around her. The attic was just packed with things! Covered with cobwebs and dust were old trunks of clothes that had been out of style many years before Margie was born. Mountains of yellowing newspapers were piled on the floor. Margie looked at one paper — it was dated 1897! There were piles of old photographs too. Most had become brown and faded. But they still showed men and women and children wearing clothes like those in the attic. There were even pictures of pet dogs and cats. Who had lived in this old house before Margie's family moved in?

Suddenly Margie caught sight of a large painting that stood against the attic wall. The painting showed a well-dressed gentleman about 60 years old. But there was nothing nice or friendly about the look on his face. His piercing gray eyes and thin mouth seemed to be alive.

And he was looking straight at Margie! For a moment, she wanted to run as far away as she could. Then she pulled her thoughts together again. How could a *picture* be alive?

And just then, she saw something else in a shadowy corner of the attic. A big wooden trunk was hiding there in the dark. What was inside it? Treasure! It had to be!

She went over to the trunk. It was bound with thick rope, but the rope was old. It was easy to pull it away. The lock had broken open many years before. Margie only had to lift the lid. The old lid groaned as the trunk came open . . . .

Yes, the trunk *was* full. But it was full of nothing but old packs of papers tied together. They looked like letters. And at the bottom, sticking out from under one pack, was the corner of a leather-covered diary. But there was nothing else at all. How disappointing for Margie!

She started to lower the lid — and then again she felt that cold feeling. But this time it wasn't like cold air. It was a hand of ice that took hold of the back of Margie's neck like a cold claw! She was so frightened that she couldn't cry out . . . or even move!

Then an icy wind roared from somewhere and blew

the lid of the trunk from Margie's fingers. The force of that wind opened the trunk wide again!

The first thing Margie saw inside the trunk was the leather-covered diary. It lay on top of the letters . . . . How had it moved?

Now the wind roared even louder — making a noise like a person in pain! It blew open the leather cover of the diary. The pages began to turn quickly.

And then, as suddenly as it had come up, the wind stopped. The attic was silent. The icy cold was still there, but it let go its hold on Margie's neck.

Shaking, she looked down at the diary. It had opened to the very last page. Margie read these words:

> *. . . my life is coming to a close. I am beginning to believe that I will never rest until I tell someone of my crime. Twenty years ago I let my brother go to prison for a theft that I really committed. I cannot forget the wrong I did him. His name must be cleared!*
>
> *May my unhappy spirit stay with this diary. Not until it is opened and my crime made known will I be at rest.*
>
> *Philip Thomas*

Margie was still shaking, but she knew what she had to do. She would take the diary from the trunk. And she'd make sure that the true story would be told. She reached down for the diary.

Suddenly, for the first time, sunlight came into the attic through a tiny window. The strange cold gave way to a soft summer breeze.

As Margie picked up the diary, she heard a sound behind her. But this time it did not frighten her. She knew it had to be a long sigh of relief.

No longer afraid to turn around, Margie looked straight at the painting. Sunlight was shining on it now. Margie was sure that the hard eyes had become softer. Around the edges of the thin, tight mouth was a little smile.

Margie looked even closer at the painting. At the very bottom, on the frame, was a small silver plate. The plate had words written on it . . .

PHILIP THOMAS, 1832-1901.

Chapter 2

Ghosts on Parade

Not everybody, of course, would believe the story of Margie and the ghost of Philip Thomas. They might say that Margie just had a lively imagination or that she dreamed it all.

But throughout history many other people have believed that ghosts are real. Some of these believers have been well-known scholars who couldn't be called dreamers!

Among those who believe in a "spirit world" are the men and women known as ghost hunters. These people study the history, actions, and personalities of ghosts all over the world. There is nothing about ghosts that ghost hunters don't know.

Ghosts, they tell us, are as old as the human race. They were known to the ancient Egyptians who placed food and water in boats for those who died. They wanted to help the spirits leave this life in comfort. The early Greeks and Romans spoke with ghosts through holy men or women called oracles. Old German stories tell of ghosts who didn't haunt houses or graveyards but lived in trees!

Ghosts have appeared to the world of the living in many ways. Often they look like misty shapes and give off the smell of perfume — or some bad, sickly smell. We like to think ghosts wear bed sheets, but these are really the white clothes in which they were buried called shrouds. Shrouds can have hoods to cover the otherworldly faces. Or ghosts might just wear the same clothes they had on while they were alive.

And because ghosts like to do mischief, they can surprise us by taking the shape of any animal that lives on the earth — and some that don't!

Another kind of ghost is never seen. It lets you know it's there by rattling chains or moaning or screaming. And sometimes people hear the sound of heavy feet in an empty hall.

Sometimes a ghost will even speak out loud. But chances are you will not be able to understand what it says.

There are also ghosts who do more than just make noise. They seem to like to bother people. Ghost

Could this broken door be the work of a *poltergeist*?

hunters call them *poltergeists*. Many people say they have seen chairs and tables flying across rooms, windows opening, doors banging shut, and books leaping up from shelves. One of the strangest stories came from a group of people who said they watched salt and pepper fly out of their shakers. The salt and pepper then mixed together in the air, came apart, and returned to the shakers!

Ghosts can surprise the living by appearing in the most unusual places!

Some spirit creatures, like gnomes, move around. But ghosts seldom travel. They usually stay in one place — a graveyard, a castle, a palace, or a house. Often ghosts stay put for hundreds of years and even longer! They haunt one place because each ghost needs something. Perhaps it wants to confess its crime like the ghost Margie met.

14

Often ghosts haunt a place because they have something they want to tell someone. But a ghost could also be waiting for something bad to happen to a descendant of a person who harmed it during its life. There are some who believe that ghosts can hurt the living. But the most ghosts have ever done is to give people a good scare!

Once the ghost has gotten what it wants, it will almost certainly leave. But not always. Some ghosts are said to haunt houses just because they had liked living there. They don't want to leave a place where they were once happy.

Because of all these different kinds of ghosts, ghost stories came into being. Many people like to tell them or read them. Some are funny, some are sad, some are scary. And some are even said to be true.

Are they?

Let's try to find out.

Chapter 3

The Haunted Gallery

Ghost hunters say that no country on earth is without ghosts. But some seem to have more ghosts than others. England may be the most "haunted" place of all. It is one of the world's oldest countries, and its many old castles and palaces make perfect homes for ghosts. Some English ghosts were just ordinary people during life, but most came from the upper classes.

One of them, in fact, was a queen of England!

And if you visit England, you can go straight to the place where this royal ghost is said to be.

Hampton Court Palace is one of the most beautiful in the world — and one of the most mysterious. It is very great and grand. Its red brick walls circle around hundreds of large rooms. There are throne rooms, audience chambers, eating halls, dressing rooms, and chapels. There are also many dark halls, galleries, and hidden stairs. Hampton Court's lovely gardens have

paths that wind through hedges more than six feet high. These hedges are the well-known "Hampton Court maze." People have been lost in it for hours.

The front door of Hampton Court is watched over by strange and fierce-looking stone animals. They are called "the king's beasts." People who visit the palace wonder what stories these strange stone animals might tell — if they could speak.

Certainly the beasts must know about the ghost!

In the year 1529, England's King Henry VIII made Hampton Court a royal palace. Years later he married the fifth of his six wives, 20-year-old Catherine Howard. Henry was almost old enough to be Catherine's grandfather! But Catherine loved her husband. She also enjoyed the power and privileges of being queen. She seemed perfectly suited to the rich life of Hampton Court.

Presently, however, Catherine's happiness began to disappear. Henry fell sick. He had always gotten angry easily, but now his moods became darker and even angrier. Catherine found that she no longer enjoyed his company.

She also found herself lonely. And her loneliness drove her to look for other company. This was not wise for a queen of England — and it was very dangerous! The king had enemies who would leap at a chance to spread stories of a secret romance. Henry's second wife, Anne Boleyn, had been beheaded because such stories had been told about her too!

It was not long before the stories reached Henry's ears. Even before she knew it, Catherine was in great danger.

Henry learned the news about his queen's supposed secret while at prayers in Hampton Court Palace. Thomas Cranmer, the archbishop of Canterbury,

King Henry VIII brought his young wife Catherine Howard to live at Hampton Court.

entered the king's chapel and handed a note to the king. Henry knew the note must have been important. Not even the archbishop of Canterbury wanted to risk making the king angry. It was well known that Henry hated to be bothered when saying his prayers.

19

A frightening silence came over the chapel as the king read the note. Henry's face went white and the note shook in his hand. Again he read the charges against his beautiful young queen.

At first Henry felt hurt. His voice shaking, he asked Cranmer if the news in the note was true. But he knew already. Cranmer was a holy man — he would not bring a false charge.

Henry's hurt feelings soon changed. He quickly became so angry he could hardly catch his breath. Still he kept his feelings from ruling him long enough to give Cranmer a command. He spoke in a voice so soft it could hardly be heard. But his voice was also scary!

"Let the queen be held in her room," said Henry, "until I decide what to do." He himself would ride off alone for a while. When he returned, he would say what he wanted to do about Catherine.

There could be no doubt what Henry VIII would decide!

The order had been given. Bowing to his king, Cranmer left the chapel. Henry turned back to his prayers. His face was still white and shaken.

By now Catherine had heard about the charges against her. She remembered what had happened to

Henry VIII read the charges against his queen while at prayers in the Chapel Royal.

Anne Boleyn. So she made up her mind to see the king right away. She knew he was still in his chapel. Surely she could make Henry believe that the charges were made by people who hated her — and him.

She must not wait another second! Catherine started for the door of her room.

Then she stopped short. Heavy footsteps sounded outside in the hall. The palace guards! They had been sent to take Catherine away, or make her a prisoner in her room.

If she did not act at this moment, it would be too late. She *must* get to the chapel to see the king. It was her only chance!

Catherine threw open the door. The guards stood in her way. She pulled herself up like the proud queen she was. How could they! How could they stand in the path of a *queen* of England!

The guards were not moved. They took orders only from Henry. They knew Catherine's rule had come to an end. To them, she was no longer queen of England but merely Catherine Howard — a young woman who would soon die!

And now, for the first time, Catherine herself did not feel like a queen. She was suddenly very

frightened. Reaching the king was all that mattered. Quickly, before the guards could stop her, she pushed past them and ran!

For a few seconds the guards looked at each other in surprise. But very soon they were ready to act. They had to be. Knowing too well what their king would do to them if they didn't catch Catherine, they ran after her.

Catherine was gasping and crying, and her heart pounded like a hammer as she raced through the halls toward the chapel. Just as she was ready to collapse, she finally reached the chapel's outer gallery. She was so close that she could even hear the king at his prayers.

Just a few more steps and her life might be spared!

She reached for the handle on the chapel door. Suddenly she felt hands catching her by the arms. The guards had run even faster than she had.

The two guards held Catherine back and asked her to act as a great lady should. Instead, she fell to her knees and pleaded. Would they not let her just take the few steps that would bring her to the king? Was that so great a thing to ask?

In answer, the guards only held Catherine's arms more tightly. They were not going to risk their own lives by letting her take even one step.

Catherine could no longer hold back the terror that was coming over her. The quiet of the gallery was broken like glass as Catherine Howard screamed!

She screamed again. And again . . . and still again.
She could not stop! All the halls of Hampton Court
Palace echoed back her continuing screams.

Once again the guards were taken by surprise. For a
second they let go of Catherine. Still screaming, she
dashed for the chapel door — only to be caught again!
One of the guards clapped his heavy hand over her
mouth. Suddenly the screaming was stopped.

Now the only sound in the gallery was the scraping of Catherine's shoes on the floor as the guards began leading her back to her room.

She had lost her one chance. In less than five minutes, the queen of England had become a prisoner — in her own palace!

The king must have heard the screaming outside his chapel. But he gave no sign of it. Soon after, he left Hampton Court — and never saw Catherine Howard again.

Catherine was sent to the Tower of London. On a field called Tower Green, the executioner brought her life to an end. The "king's beasts" outside Hampton Court Palace had seen and heard the last of Catherine Howard.

Or had they?

Soon after Catherine died, people began calling the little gallery outside the king's chapel by a special name. To this very day it is known by that name.

It is called the Haunted Gallery.

Over the past 500 years, a ghostly shape is said to have appeared often at Hampton Court. It has been seen racing toward Henry VIII's chapel.

This ghost has not only been seen — it has been heard! From the gallery outside the chapel, loud screams are said to ring again through the palace halls. And then suddenly the screams stop, just as if a hand were placed over the screamer's mouth! Hampton Court falls silent again.

Is it hard to guess who the ghost is? Who else could it be but Catherine Howard? Doesn't it seem that she

Some say that Catherine Howard's cries for help still echo through the Haunted Gallery.

still wishes to plead her case to Henry VIII, hoping he might yet be moved to spare her?

Or is the ghost only imagined by those who visit the palace and hear the story of Catherine Howard?

Ask "the king's beasts."

Chapter 4

The Ghost of Octagon House

James Madison was president of the United States from 1809 to 1817. And in Washington, D.C., the country's capital, there was no one people liked better than Madison's charming and friendly wife, Dolly.

James and Dolly Madison often visited with friends in a famous, oddly-shaped brick house called Octagon House. Later this graceful mansion would be their home. It was near the White House, and both houses were joined by a secret tunnel under the ground. Dolly Madison felt as much at home in Octagon House as in the White House. And she also knew about the secret tunnel.

But little did she know that one day she would need that tunnel — very badly!

In 1812 the United States and England were at war once again. The fierce fighting even reached Washington, where the Capitol and the White House were taken by the British and set on fire!

In both the Capitol and the White House were important papers and works of art. They would be lost forever if nothing was done to save them.

Some Americans were so frightened that they thought only of saving themselves. They ran from the burning buildings — but with empty hands.

But there were others who thought of their country. Dolly Madison was one of them. There was no way she could reach the Capitol. But as she watched the fire near the walls of the White House, she remembered the tunnel.

And she decided to try to save at least one of America's greatest treasures — the picture of George Washington that had been painted by Gilbert Stuart nearly 20 years earlier.

While the guns roared all around, Dolly Madison went down to the cellar of Octagon House and entered the tunnel. She was going to do a dangerous job!

Though others ran from the burning buildings with empty hands, Dolly Madison saved important papers and works of art.

James and Dolly Madison lived in Octagon House after the White House burned down in 1814.

Dolly Madison was frightened — and well she might be! British troops were very near Octagon House. At any moment they might break in, rush to the cellar — and find the tunnel!

The tunnel was close and wet and dark. Dolly

Madison had only a small candle to light her way —
and to keep off the rats.

Maybe it would be best to turn back!

But Dolly Madison had made up her mind, and she
was not about to give up.

She pushed on through the tunnel, tripping now
and then in the dark. At every second she thought she
was just about to hear the order "Halt!" — or the
sound of a British gun. If she did, it would be the last
sound she would ever hear!

But she reached the White House. There was still a
chance to save the painting — and not get caught by
the British!

By now the White House was on fire. But Dolly
Madison was able to make her way upstairs to the
room where Washington's picture hung. Quickly she
took it from the wall and also gathered up some
important papers from a desk. Then she ran down the
burning stairs and into the secret tunnel.

The tunnel was not long. But now Dolly Madison
was loaded down with the heavy painting and the
papers she had saved. It seemed as if she had miles yet
to go! She kept moving though. Suddenly the candle
blew out, and the tunnel went black!

At last she saw a little light ahead. It was the cellar of Octagon House. Only a few steps to go!

She stopped . . . and almost fainted . . . .

There was a noise up ahead!

The British! They had found the tunnel! Now she could not go ahead or turn back. She was trapped! She got ready to die.

But then she remembered what she was carrying. She could not bear the idea of George Washington's picture falling into the hands of the enemy.

So she started on again — and tripped. She screamed as the painting fell to the ground with a crash!

That scream probably helped her pull herself together. She now realized that the noise she heard might not have been the British at all! It was probably just a rat.

And there, only a step away, was the cellar door of Octagon House. Tired, frightened, and almost crying, Dolly Madison picked up the painting and entered the cellar.

But just to be safe, she closed and locked the cellar door. If any of the British were in the tunnel, they could just stay there until later!

Then Dolly Madison took a deep breath and smiled. She had saved the painting. It would belong forever to her fellow Americans!

Nearly 180 years have gone by since Dolly Madison saved the picture of George Washington. Octagon House still stands. And many people think that there is someone invisible living in its cellar! From time to time, it is said, the smell of lilacs suddenly fills the house. Then, only seconds later, a scream is heard in the cellar — followed right away by a crash!

Ghost hunters think that Dolly Madison has come back to Octagon House to act out again her frightening scene. First comes the smell of the flowers Dolly loved. Then her frightened cry rings out in the tunnel. The painting falls to the ground . . . and then there is silence.

Once again Dolly Madison is safe.

But why does this gentle ghost keep returning to live through those scary seconds in the tunnel — over and over and over again? She can hardly enjoy remembering the scare she got when she thought she

Dolly Madison
used the secret tunnel
to save Gilbert Stuart's
painting of George Washington.

had fallen into an enemy trap. That's the kind of thing people like to forget!

Then why does she come back?

Could it be that Dolly Madison wants to live over her moment of victory? She must have felt proud when she knew that she was safe — and that she had saved one of America's greatest treasures.

That would be a feeling worth having again many, many times!

Guest House for Ghosts

Ghosts don't move around much. Probably Dolly Madison's ghost would never get to California. But if it did, it would feel right at home in one of the strangest houses on earth ... *A house built specially for visiting ghosts!*

This story begins with a gun.

In 1866 Oliver Fisher Winchester invented the Winchester rifle. It became one of the best-known guns in the West. Many great figures of the Old West — Buffalo Bill, Annie Oakley, and Butch Cassidy — carried Winchesters. The rifle was also used to fight Indians. It has even been called "the gun that won the West."

By 1888, Oliver Winchester and his son had both died. His son's wife, Sarah, inherited all the Winchesters' money.

And Sarah Winchester was frightened.

She was afraid of the spirits of the people who had been killed by Winchester rifles. With her husband and father-in-law gone, she believed that many ghosts would now come after her.

Sarah was most afraid of the Indians' ghosts. Maybe she would have been less worried if she knew many Indians had Winchesters. When Sitting Bull defeated General Custer at the Little Bighorn in 1876, the Indians carried Winchesters, but the soldiers didn't!

But Sarah didn't know this. So she went to a medium.

A medium is a person who says he or she can talk to those in the spirit world. And Sarah's medium told her that she was right to be afraid. Yes, the ghosts would never give Winchester's daughter-in-law an easy moment. Hundreds of Indians would haunt her. So would many others! ... Unless she could find a way to stop them!

But how?

The medium had a plan.

He explained that there were two kinds of ghosts. Some meant harm, but others were only looking for a place where they could find rest. Sarah was told to build a home for the friendly ghosts. They in turn

would protect her from the others — the bad ghosts!

But it was most important, said the medium, to build the house with the help of the friendly ghosts. They would make their wishes known to Sarah.

41

Ghosts were about to design their own house!

And Sarah Winchester would be safe as long as the sounds of building could be heard in the house. The medium explained that the ghosts wanted their house to continue growing. Maybe it would *never* be finished!

Sarah was willing to obey these orders from the "other world." But she did not build from the ground up. Instead, she bought a large house that was already standing near San Jose, California. Then she lost no time getting builders to add new rooms and even whole new wings. Soon Sarah was known near and far as the owner of the strangest haunted house in the world, the Winchester Ghost Mansion.

As long as Sarah lived there, the sounds of the builders never stopped. There were no Sundays off, no days of rest. The spirits would not allow them. And so through the years the strange house never stopped growing!

When Sarah Winchester first bought the house it had 18 rooms. For her ghostly friends she added *130* more rooms! Even the kings and queens of Hampton Court Palace were not taken care of as well as the spirits who lived in the Ghost Mansion.

Knowing that ghosts don't have shadows, Sarah Winchester thought they might feel unhappy if they saw

hers. She explained this to the builders, and they set up the lights so that no shadows ever appeared anywhere in the whole house!

There was also the problem of mirrors. Ghosts don't show up in mirrors. And again Sarah tried to please. In all the 130 rooms only *two* mirrors were to be found!

Sarah knew too that fireplaces are used by ghosts to enter the world of living people. To make sure that her ghosts did not have to wait or take turns, she had *50* fireplaces put in at Ghost Mansion!

43

Ghosts like to be on time, not one second early or one second late. Some of Sarah Winchester's ghosts always came just as the clock rang midnight. Others liked to come in one hour later. Almost always they would leave at two o'clock in the morning . . . exactly!

How could Sarah be sure the ghosts would know the exact time?

She had a bell tower put up. Sarah let only two of the people who worked for her ring the bells. Sarah gave these people the best clocks and pocket watches that money could buy. The clocks told the time right down to the second! At *exactly* midnight, at *exactly* 1:00 A.M., and at *exactly* 2:00 A.M., the great bells of the Winchester Ghost Mansion could be heard all around the neighborhood. No spirit-friend of Sarah's ever had to ask what time it was!

Every so often the living owner of Ghost Mansion held meetings with her guests the ghosts so they could give her their orders about work on the house. Meetings with ghosts are called seances, and Sarah Winchester had a seance room. It was quite different from the rest of the house. All the other rooms had rich, comfortable furniture. There was nothing in this tiny room except for one table and one chair. On the table were the paper and pen with which Sarah wrote down the words of her ghost-guests.

The bell tower helped the ghosts enter and leave Ghost Mansion at their favorite hour.

The seance room was also Sarah's best kept secret. The smartest detectives in the world might never have sniffed it out! Sarah had a good reason for keeping the room hidden. She didn't want enemy ghosts to discover it! Remember, she had built Ghost Mansion to keep away the angry spirits of those who had been killed by the Winchester rifle. The friendly ghosts would help protect her, but it would still be dangerous for their enemies to find the room where she met with her friends!

This room was not the only secret of Ghost Mansion. Sarah Winchester tricked bad spirits in many other ways. The builders must have scratched their heads in surprise at some of the strange plans they were given. Many stairs, for example, led to doors that could not be opened. Other stairs had seven flights — but hardly went higher than a man's head. Each step was only two inches high! Surely that would baffle any enemy spirits who found their way into Ghost Mansion!

Doors were built so that they could be opened only from the outside. When closed, they could not be opened from the inside. That was just the way to trap a ghost bent on doing harm.

And that wasn't all. Balconies that looked large really were not. They seemed to grow smaller as you walked onto them. One could enter the house easily through large windows — only to find dozens of doors. Some were locked. Others led nowhere. Ghost Mansion, in fact, was one big maze! By the time an enemy spirit found a way in, Sarah Winchester could be safe in her room.

And even that room was protected against spirits. One of its doors was not a real door. Another opened into the seance room. But it did not open *out* from that room! A smaller door served as the exit. It would have been dangerous for a hurrying spirit to use that door. For Sarah had put a bar across it 18 inches above the floor. Any spirit going through that small door would have tripped over the bar!

To keep herself safe, Sarah Winchester left nothing to chance. Today some people believe that the number 13 is not lucky. But in Sarah's time 13 was thought to bring bad luck only to bad people. So that number helped Sarah fight her ghostly enemies! Thirteen glass balls were put on every chandelier in Ghost Mansion. There were 13 panels in each wall. And nearly all the stairs had 13 steps. It was enough to make any bad spirit think again before trying to harm the owner of the house!

Sarah Winchester spent a lot of money on Ghost Mansion. Did it do her any good?

Who can tell? All we know is that she lived there happily until 1922 when she died at age 87. She had spent nearly 40 years in a haunted house.

And during those years, without stopping for a single day, builders had been working on the house. Always they had followed orders that came from the lips of ghosts! But on the day Sarah died, the sounds of building stopped. The builders' job was finished.

Sarah Winchester's home can be seen today. It is a California State landmark.

And people who come to visit the big house can be sure they have come to the right place.

Thirteen trees line the driveway.

What Do You Think?

We have met them now — queenly ghosts, patriotic ghosts, angry ghosts, ghosts with stories to tell, noisy ghosts, silent ghosts, ghosts that could not be seen — and ghosts that could be seen all too well!

Their presence can't be explained. Many people are certain that there is nothing at all *to* explain. There's just no such thing as a ghost, they say.

And this could be so. After all, no one has ever proved that ghosts exist.

But no one has ever proved that they don't!